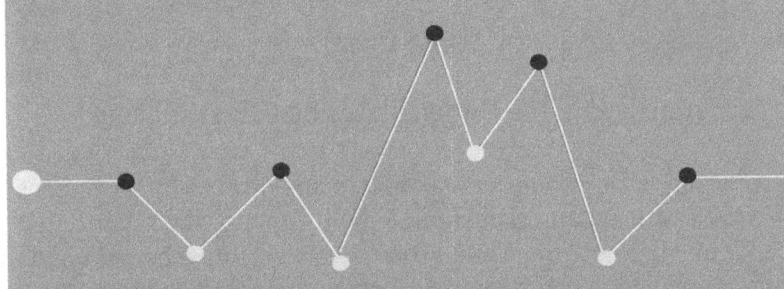

simplifyism

Connecting the Dots through
Simplicity

G. Eb Williams

Ordering Information
For additional copies contact support@simplifyism.com. Quantity discounts are available.

ISBN-13: 978-1903060252
ISBN-10: 1983868256

Printed in the United States of America.

Cover, book art design, illustrations, and jacket design by G. Eb Williams.

First Edition

www.simplifyism.com

Dedicated to Mom, Auntie Darrylin and Yonie

You Simplify Everything that is Meaningful to me.
Thank you for your unconditional love and support.

Contents

Disclaimer:

The information in this book is provided for general informational purposes only. No information contained in this book should be construed as legal advice or legal information from the individual author, nor is it intended to be a substitute for legal counsel on any subject matter. No reader of this book should act or refrain from acting on the basis of any information included in, or accessible through, this book without first seeking legal counsel or other appropriate professional advice regarding your own unique situation. Furthermore, this book does not encourage nor promote any illegal, unethical, nor harmful activities. Reading this book, or using information from it, does not create an attorney-client relationship between you and the author. If you do need to hire an attorney, the hiring of a lawyer is an important decision that should not be based solely upon advertisements. Before you decide, ask the attorney(s) to send you free written information about their qualifications and experience.

G. Eb Williams

INTRODUCTION

1. What is Simplifyism?

Definition:

Simplifyism: *sim•pli•fy•ism* (a noun)

Simplifyism can be defined as *a method and a mindset of exercising one's ability to focus, connect, and process complex information, ideas, and occurrences into their simplest form.*[1]

Origin:

Simplifyism is a word created by the author, G. Eb Williams. This word is not in the U.S. dictionary, as of yet, but hopefully someday it will be in the U.S. dictionary.

Purpose:

The purpose of Simplifyism is to provide insight to improving productivity and time-management through simplicity.

---

[1] Simplifyism, and its definition, applies to general information, ideas, and occurrences. Simplifyism, and its definition, does not apply to legal information, legal ideas or legal matters.

Perspective:

Simplifyism is about a perspective, rather than a promise. Simplifyism does not imply solutions to all life's problems and circumstances one may encounter. Rather, it is more a resource and a message that assists one to embrace the uncertainty and complexity of life's journey as creative catalysts and opportunities.

Simplifyism is not just about what you can do without or what you can relinquish; however, it is more about what you can do with what you already have, even if there is not an excess of things and information. Some people do not have access to a vast amount of information or technology. Furthermore, some people do not have money, nor materialistic things or physical items in the first place to give away.

Simplifyism is about focusing on what you *do* have, and what you can *create* from what you already have. We have a tendency to underutilize the options, skills and resources we do have and think only with a consumer mindset, rather than a creator mindset. What if for just one moment, you are able to use creativity to create a solution, rather than just solely consume a problem?[2] You would be surprised at not only your

---

[2] What this means is creating an ethical solution that could help others and add genuine value to other's lives. Meaning not an illegal or unethical solution.

options, but also your potential and the value you can provide for others, as well.

Simplifyism is about determining what works best for you by utilizing your existing resources, skills and strengths. It is up to you, your choice, your time, your decision, and your option to determine what works best for you. If you are looking for better productivity, this book presents different options and approaches. However, it is ultimately up to you to choose and adopt the best approach that serves your mindset, pace and circumstances the best.

This book may not be useful if you feel your life is already simple or easily manageable. If your life is filled with fulfilling, meaningful activities, you are focused and progressing at the pace you want, then you may not need all of the information provided in this book. If you feel overloaded, distracted, unproductive and not progressing at the rate that you wish, you may find this book of interest and insightful. Overall, Simplifyism provides a fresh perspective of living with more focus and design, instead of living by distraction and default.

Relevancy:

Simplifyism is universally relevant at this time. Today, we live in a world and an era of overconsumption and over sharing of information, which creates a lot of noise in our society. Some of this information is interesting, thus having a magnetic quality that attracts our attention. However, it also creates more complexity within that information that is not easily comprehended.

Currently, there is a problem with this overconsumption of information. We are being blasted with tons of information from multiple sources. Moreover, information is being poured into our eyes effortlessly through the Internet. Technology generally, and the Internet specifically, both have influenced this overconsumption complication. This overconsumption has impacted how we learn and process a vast amount of information. The Internet and technology both can be viewed as a double-edge sword. On one side, both have changed how we communicate, view and store information, which makes all information accessible; However, on the other side, both have made us extremely reliant on technology and mobile devices as methods by which we communicate and consume information. With this reliance and the more accessibility to information, complexity has increased rapidly due to the information overload and overconsumption of numerous opinions, data, concepts, and processes. So how do we as human beings learn to focus, connect and process this vast amount of diverse information and not get stuck down the rabbit hole of complexities and overconsumption?

Method:

Simplifyism encompasses and concentrates on the following method: 1. *Focusing* on what you already do have and what is most meaningful, 2. *Connecting* one idea to another, and 3. *Processing* complex matter. This book helps you perform an in-depth analysis on: How you *focus, connect, and process* complex information, ideas and occurrences in this chaotic world.

NOTE: *The method of Simplifyism does NOT apply to any legal methods, legal matters, legal information, legal ideas, or any legal occurrences. The method of Simplifyism does not guarantee any solutions.*

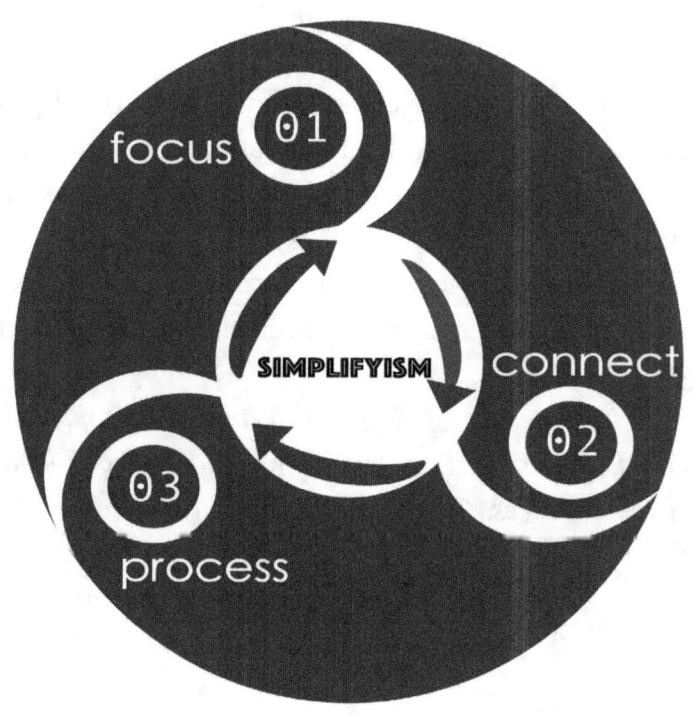

Part I: FOCUS

Focus On What You Already Do Have and What Is Most Meaningful

Focus allows us to connect and process information, ideas and occurrences. Our ability to focus is essential to conquering complexities. Whether these complexities are within or derived from information, ideas or occurrences, our ability to focus on what we already do have and what is most meaningful will allow us to maximize our potential by giving our highest concentration and contribution to the matter.

Focus enables us to utilize our power to discern the substantive from the useless, and look past the extraneous detail. In turn, we gain better understanding and clarity of the important detail, which others overlook. The concept of focus seems pretty simple, but as we dive into what focus really encompasses and requires, it is not as clear. In fact, more intense concentration and effort is actually required in order to focus.

For instance, say you are walking outside after it has rained. As you are walking, you look up in the sky and a rainbow appears. You glance up at the rainbow, while walking, and then you take your eyes off it immediately and continue with your walk.

Now let's take a look at another scenario, say as you are walking outside, you look up in the sky and a rainbow appears. You stop, pause and take notice of the rainbow. You look at the rainbow a little bit more. You reach into your pocket and pull out your smart phone, which has a camera installed in it. You open the camera application, zoom in and take a picture.

In the second instance, you not only performed an action directly related to the subject by stopping, but you also performed an action directly related to the subject by taking a picture, as well. It is that simple. This is what focus is, in comparison to a passing glance. As you see, focus is deeper than a glance. When you focus on something, you are giving it your undivided attention even if it is for a minute. In addition, when you focus, you sometimes perform an action directly related to the subject. In comparison, when you glance at something, you are not giving it your undivided attention. Moreover, when you glance at something, you do not perform an action directly related to the subject.

Let's go a little deeper into the focus analysis. What made you focus in on the rainbow? The rainbow was probably beautiful and captivated your eyes. But what made you stop, act, and take a picture of the rainbow? There was a motivating factor that caused you to stop, reach into your pocket, and take the picture. That motivation could have been the need to capture the rainbow image for a tangible memory or storage for your future memory for further review. Maybe you wanted to share the rainbow with others through texting or emailing it, or posting it on your timeline etc. *Purpose* is what made you stop and go deeper to focus on taking and recording the picture of the rainbow. Purpose is the motivating factor and direction that determines your focus.

G. Eb Williams

Purpose

Try to start each day with focus and follow through with actions that align with your purpose.

Focus begins with a purpose, plain and simple. Now finding your purpose and living with purpose is more of a challenge, which requires time, concentrated effort, prioritizing and action. Purpose is the motivating factor for why you are taking such action. Whether it is your purpose in life, or a goal oriented purpose, in order to successfully focus, connect, and process information and ideas, there needs to be a defined purpose, resulting in action.

Your purpose is a navigational tool to help give you direction and guide your life. When you do discover your purpose, celebrate and embrace it, because every successful result begins with a purpose. Your purpose creates tolerance for the unknown and is your strength to persevere.

Moreover, your purpose is what you build upon to connect the dots. The key is to focus on the elements in your life that do align with your purpose. Sift and filter out the elements in your life that do not align with your purpose. To assist you in determining which elements to focus on and sift out, perform an assessment of what is most meaningful to you in your life. This assessment is what I like to call the *VEINS* assessment.

> **When your purpose is clear, perform the VEINS assessment to help you stay aligned with your particular purpose.**

First, lets examine how veins work in your body. Veins are any one of the tubes that carry blood from various parts of the body back to the heart, thus forming part of the blood circulatory system of the body. Veins are crucial to keeping you alive and breathing. Veins are tricky because you can see some of them on the outer surface of the body (the skin) but you cannot see their internal operation. Veins can be seen on just about anything living, such as on the surface of a leaf, on the wing of an insect, and even on the ears of a dog.

In the context of this assessment, *VEINS* stands for the following terms: **V**aluable, **E**ssential, **I**mportant, **N**ecessary and **S**ubstantive (*VEINS*). Take the time and determine what is MOST: Valuable, Essential, Important, Necessary and Substantive (*VEINS*) in your life. Similar to how veins keep blood moving and flowing throughout your body, performing the *VEINS* assessment keeps you moving and flowing towards focusing on and fulfilling your purpose. Determining what is most Valuable, Essential, Important, Necessary and Substantive in your life keeps you focused on what truly matters in your life. Lets take a look at each term very closely and in more depth because they are all connected and related to one another. These five terms overlap one another, but they all focus on how you can cultivate and prioritize your skills, time and relationships.

    a. *Valuable*: The worth or usefulness of something. In addition, it can refer to a person's principles, values or standards of behavior. Examine your values and behavior from time to time. In whatever task you are performing, examine if it aligns with your purpose and values. Also, evaluate if what you are doing is useful to others or to yourself.

    b. *Essential*: Absolutely vital or key. Examine what is essential to helping you function on a daily basis. Evaluate what is needed for your basic survival.

    c. *Important*: Having a great significance. Examine which relationships, commitments, tasks and habits are important to achieving your daily or long-term goals.

    d. *Necessary*: Obligatory or required in order to achieve a particular result. Examine the necessary tools and mechanisms you need and use on a daily basis. Evaluate the necessary steps in order to achieve your goals and fulfill your purpose.

e. *Substantive*: That which is meaningful or considerable. Examine what is a meaningful or considerable use of your time.

Examining these terms (*VEINS*) from time to time can help you refocus on your purpose and determine what truly matters in your life. This assessment helps you structure your life around simplicity.

When you focus on your purpose, pay attention to what is most meaningful to you. In addition, identify and embrace the resources, relationships and skills you already do have that support your purpose. Your purpose is the foundation you can build upon to help others and add value to this world. Examine your daily habits and activities to see if they are aligning with your purpose. This aids in shaping your focus to continue on your path to fulfill your purpose and creating the *time* for carrying out your purpose.

Time

Everyone has a purpose, but time waits for no one.

When you determine what is most meaningful to you, you can focus on your purpose and prioritize your time to fulfill your purpose. You may have discovered your purpose in life, but if you do not take the time to focus on it or tune into it, how are you going to live with purpose? Purpose without taking the *time* to focus on it or tune into it, is powerless.

Focus encompasses your ability to give undivided, concentrated effort and attention to a task that aligns with your purpose. In order to have that undivided, concentrated effort on your personal goals and tasks, you have to carve out time for it. Not only do you have to carve out time for it, but you have to protect and guard that time, as well.

Carving out Time

If a thing is worth doing, it is worth doing well. If it is worth having, it is worth waiting for. If it is worth attaining, it is worth fighting for. If it is worth experiencing, it is worth putting aside time for.
- Oliver Wilde

You will find great things happen when you invest time into the progression of yourself. Part of this investment entails carving out time for yourself in order to fully focus on developing your gifts and talents, so you can best serve others. When you carve out time for yourself, you are investing in yourself by developing an understanding of the value and potential that you possess that is worth giving the time, energy and space to enhance.

Taking the time to invest in yourself is one of the best returns on investments you can have. Whether it's tuning into your purpose, expanding your knowledge by learning a new skill, or developing yourself personally or professionally, carve out time to invest in yourself. If you think about it, you invest your money, trust and time in multiple companies on a daily basis. You invest in someone else's companies through their products and services. Whether it is purchasing lunch at a restaurant or it is working for another person's company, you are investing in someone else's business. Some people even invest in the stock market. So the question is why not also

24

invest time, energy and money in yourself? When you work for someone else's company, the company is paying you and thus, helping you fund or enhance your own success either through experience, skills or monetary compensation. Sometimes your own success is dependent on another's success. When you are investing in other companies' products, services and ultimately its ability to be successful, try to also take the time to ask yourself the following question: When I invest in other companies' products or services, is this investment also contributing to my own ability to be successful, as well?

As humans, we are very habitual and routine. We all have some necessary routines we cannot afford to do without. We have habitual routines and traps that soak up our energy and time, to the very last digit. Speaking of digits, lets look more at numbers and specifically, breaking down a day into its simplest form for more context.

There are approximately 24 hours in a day, 1,440 minutes in a day and 86,400 seconds in a day. Now lets take a look at Monday through Friday, because that is where most of our time is demanded and are the busiest days of the week. If you work full-time for someone else, or go to school full-time Monday through Friday, then eight hours of your day is spent either working for someone else or attending classes all day. Also take into consideration, the time commuting to and from work or school, having lunch and socializing with peers. Then take into consideration another eight hours for sleeping and resting. Also take note that some time may be allocated for spending time with your family. This equates to eight hours remaining in the work or school day to work on your personal goals with undivided, concentrated effort and attention. That is a generous estimate by the way, because life happens and there are other mandatory tasks that occur daily.

It is hard to achieve that perfect work/life balance, because of all the disproportionate time we spend on multitasking each and every day. Most of us have a job where we work the "standard" work week consisting of five eight-hour days, commonly served between 9:00 am to 5:00 pm or 10:00 am to 6:00 pm. In addition, most of us have at least an hour commute to and from work each day. When we do arrive at the job, our time is automatically in the hands of our employer. Most likely our time and attention is devoted to performing the work we were hired for. Not only is our time utilized at the job, but also our physical and mental energy is soaked up at the job, as well. At the end of the day, when we do arrive at home after working eight hours at the job, we are tired and need some time to decompress and relax.

Most of us do not have 100% autonomy over our time. However, we do have some level or degree of control of our downtime. Even if it is a little bit of downtime, we can choose how we utilize that time. It is hard but we have to make some sacrifices. Whatever we decide to devote our time to, we are sacrificing something else. For instance, if one wanted to devote more time to start or develop his or her own business, they're going to have to reduce the time they spend on their personal hobbies in order to carve out some time to devote to their business.

In order to focus and work on your personal goals, you have to carve out time for yourself. In carving out time for yourself, try to start out with a small block of thirty minutes a day. Once you can handle thirty minutes a day, try to build a momentum and establish a rhythm of up to an hour. Once you can adjust to an hour a day, work toward increasing hours per day in thirty-minute increments. The goal is to start with small, thirty-minute time blocks and build increments at your own pace. Ideally, try to build up to four hours per day in thirty-minute increments. However, even two hours a day can make a difference. Carving out this time for yourself is important because it teaches you the value of your own time. When you do decide to invest in yourself and work on your personal goals, you have to carve out time for yourself and also guard your time, as well, in order to fully focus.

Guarding your Time

In life, you have to constantly ask yourself the following question: What is the most important use of my time and the resources I currently have? For instance, I had to ask myself this question. My answer is I believe in spending time with my loved ones and creating beautiful things. Once you figure out what is the most important use of your time, you will try to make the most of it because unlike things and money, you cannot get time back. To make the most of the time you do have, you have to learn to guard your time. In order to guard your time, it takes 1. Being Present and 2. Being Prepared.

1. Being Present

As stated before, we as humans are naturally creatures of habit and routine. To some of us, routine gives us a feeling of stability in this chaotic world. However, the big problem with routine is everything starts looking and feeling the same. If not carefully balanced, routine becomes just motion, but not momentum.

On a daily basis we go through the motions of performing repeated habits, tasks, and obligations. Within this constant repetition of routines, many of us do not take the time to evaluate if we are being present (living) in the moment or just going through the motions. This is a crucial evaluation because being present in the moment, keeps you aware of life. It keeps you aware of what is going on within you and around you. If you do not take the time to understand what is going on within you and around you, it is hard to focus, connect and process matter within your reach.

Because we are humans and humans are wired to be busy, it is sometimes hard to make the distinction of whether we are being present in the moment or going through the motions. Being aware and present in the moment requires deliberate time and focus. This type of focus entails making conscious and intentional time to comprehend what is going on within you and around you. To determine if you are being present in the moment or going through the motions, think about your everyday actions, reactions, motions and your habitual routines performed daily, monthly and even yearly.

Generally, the very first step of most daily routines begins with the act of waking up. This is the most privileged, opportunity to set the tone for the rest of your day. You are fortunate, to have the ability to rise each day. Take the deliberate time to acknowledge and be thankful for the ability to wake up each day. Rather than immediately jumping into habitual routines, take some time to slow down and focus on peaceful solitude.

When faced with an uncontrollable and unforeseeable situation or problem, take the time to stop and process your thoughts, rather than immediately reacting. Taking the time to stop and slow down, allows you to take control of your time and the situation. You are guarding your time by keeping it from being completely consumed solely by reactions, habitual routines and motions.

Some habitual routines and motions are necessary and healthy for the establishment of order in your life. It is important to implement some healthy, personal practices to create more balance in your life.

As previously stated, develop a healthy habit of scheduling time alone for you with no outside distractions. This allows for the development of self-discipline and internal focus. This could be taking the time to pray, stretch, meditate, journal, or go for a walk. Spending unrushed time with yourself in solitude, even just a little, does wonders for your sanity and peace. Whatever circumstances you may encounter, try to stop, find your inner peace and be present in the moment, rather than immediately reacting solely based on habitual routines and motions.

2. Being Prepared

Another method of guarding your time is through continuous preparation. Part of the preparation is taking the time to evaluate how you *spend* your time each day. Take a look at the actions and tasks you perform, from the time you wake up to the time you go to sleep. Make a list and jot down the tasks and activities you perform to see if they align with your purpose or goals in life. If they do not, eliminate those tasks and activities that do not align with your purpose or goals. Then try to prepare time for the tasks and activities that are most meaningful to you, the *VEINS*, in your life.

In addition, pay mind to your current, ongoing and upcoming commitments. Take the time to evaluate and prepare for your current and upcoming commitments. This may include family obligations or work commitments. Think about which commitments have to be done and which have some flexibility in completion. Evaluate which of these commitments support the *VEINS*, in your life, so you can make preparations.

All in all, when you evaluate and assess what you are doing on a daily basis it allows you to focus on what is most meaningful to you. Now, focusing on what is most meaningful when it relates solely to information can be more of a challenge. In order to focus on what is most meaningful, when it relates to information, you have to be able to distinguish the difference between substantive information and useless information.

Substantive Information vs. Useless Information[3]

We live in an era of information overload and overconsumption. There are multiple layers of information communicated through multiple mediums, such as a television, a phone, the Internet or even people. So the question is: How do we maneuver and sift through all the voluntarily and involuntarily information we encounter each day? The answer varies and depends on each individual's circumstances and life.

One layer of information you seek and consume is through the most accessible medium. This medium is technology. Through technology you are able to seek and consume information by searching through an Internet browser on a mobile device or a computer, watching a television, or texting and emailing on a mobile device or a computer. Another layer of information you seek and consume is through a non-technological medium such as, word of mouth or face-to-face interaction.

---

[3] Substantive and Useless information in the context of Simplifyism applies to general, non-legal information.

No matter what medium you intend to use, there is some necessary information you consume, which is essential to function, perform and take care of life responsibilities. This information can be grouped into three categories: 1. Personal, 2. Professional, or 3. Educational information. Some personal information you know and remember includes: phone numbers, addresses, usernames, passwords, account numbers, social security numbers, birthdates and license numbers. From a professional perspective, some information you know and remember may include usernames, passwords, programs, important deadlines, processes, procedures, and acronyms. Even from an educational standpoint, some information you know and remember may include specific course work, subject matter, outlines and test dates. These different types of necessary information are essential in taking care of life responsibilities. Overall, there are all types of information, but how do you navigate through the clutter of useless, distractive information to find the useful, substantive information?

First, you have to determine the difference between substantive information and useless information. Making this determination of which information is substantive or useless, depends on its application for each individual and his or her circumstances in life. *Substantive* information is meaningful and has a useful, value. This type of information has a foundation that is reliable. Substantive information has an important purpose or serves a purpose in your life.

On the other hand, *Useless* information is a distraction that consumes your time. There is a favorite quote by Henry David Thoreau that states, *"It's not enough to be busy; so are the ants. The question is: What are you busy about?"* When you engage in, seek or consume useless information, you should evaluate what you are sacrificing in your life in exchange for the time you spend in the consumption of useless information. Are you sacrificing relationships you can nurture, skills you can enhance or personal development in exchange for the time you spend consuming useless information?

In order to determine which information is substantive or useless, examine whether it is adding value to your purpose and life or if it is sacrificing your time and productivity in your life. In making this distinction and determination, you should ask yourself the following questions: Is this information derived from a reliable source? Will this information help others? Does this information pertain to me? Does this information add any benefit to others or myself? Is this information any of my business? Does this information serve any other purpose besides gossip? Is this information detrimental? Is this information pertinent or applicable to my life, purpose, relationships, or profession? Is this information assisting me in getting closer to my goals? Is this information serving a positive or negative influence in my life? Is there a substitute for this information?

There is certainly an influx of information. However, with all of this information, it is more about whether this information serves a purpose and is substantive? It is an art to be able to distinguish and simplify substantive information and sift out useless fluff disguised as pertinent information. Once you develop this ability, it is a valuable tool.

Think of your brain as a key chain ring. Then think of information as keys on that key chain ring. Similar to information, keys sometimes give us a level of reliability and a sense of security. Keys provide accessibility to numerous things. With the possession of the right keys you have control in locking and gaining accessibility. However, a key chain ring can fit, only so many keys on that ring. Too many keys on one key chain ring will weigh it down and make your pocket or purse heavier. Some key chain rings with too many keys on them can even prevent you from starting a car with a turnkey ignition. With too many keys on a key chain ring, you can get confused. You then have to take a further step by labeling or organizing each key to determine which key is for what use or purpose.

Take the time to check and see if your key chain ring is filled with necessary keys and/or unnecessary keys. Some necessary keys are for use in your home, office, mailbox, car, etc. All these necessary and useful keys help you function on a daily basis. However, what about those maybe extra, unnecessary keys? You may have some unnecessary and useless keys on your key chain ring that serve no purpose other than to weigh your key chain ring down. Similar to these unnecessary and useless keys on key chain rings, useless information can cloud your brain, confuse you and weigh you down, as well. As humans, we can process only so much information at one time, so it is important to make the distinction of which information is substantive or useless, to minimize confusion. Understanding this distinction, can possibly give you the keys to unlocking your potential to focus on what is most meaningful when it relates to information.

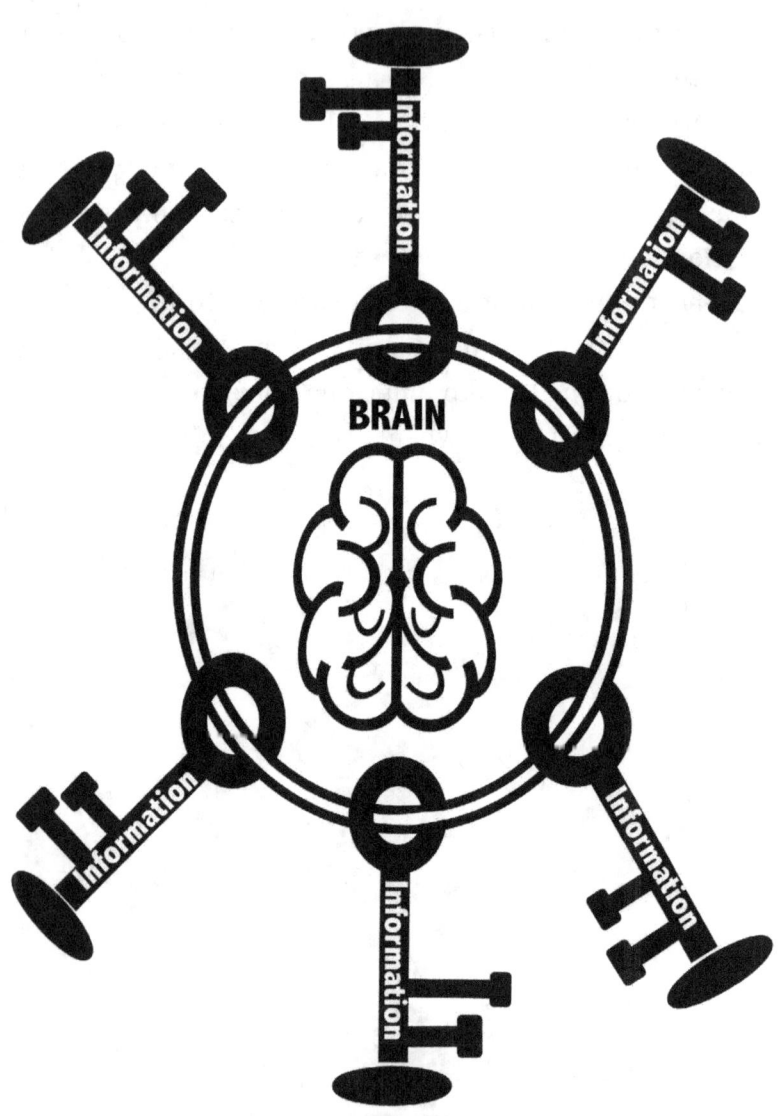

BRAIN KEY CHAIN RING of INFORMATION KEYS

Distractions

Many times we do not even know which information is substantive or useless because we are too easily distracted. We live in a busy, distracted world, let alone our own bubble of distraction. Distractions come in many forms, so it is important to recognize and evaluate how distractions operate.

Similar to you taking the time to evaluate what you are doing on a daily basis, make sure you also take the time to evaluate what is distracting you on a daily basis. These distractions may be preventing you from accomplishing your goals and focusing on what truly matters in your life.

1. Habitual Distractions

One way to look deeper at your daily habitual distractions is to evaluate which products or services have been engineered to be a dependency or to be a distraction. The Internet is engineered to be a tool to help access information, however, it is also engineered to be a dependency. Look out for the products and services itself that are engineered to be habit forming and addictive, such as social media.

Social media can distract you and take up your time if you don't pay attention to and monitor your use. Look at even the unique design features social media offers, such as a timeline. A timeline is designed to post about how you spend your time, while taking away your time literally at the same time.

We sometimes overvalue the benefits of social media and undervalue the costs of social media. Some valuable uses of social media are for professional use, keeping in touch with loved ones, locating missing people and staying informed. However, there are some costs associated with social media, such as distraction, that can be habit forming if you don't pay attention to and monitor your use.

Habits are sometimes hard to form and hard to break. Take the time to examine your habits and routines, because this aids in determining how you process and focus on information and ideas. Determine what is the *it* in hab*it* that keeps you distracted on a daily basis? Is it boredom, lack of direction or not having a clear purpose to fulfill? Habitual distractions take away the time you could be using to work and focus on your personal goals.

2. Impulsive Distractions

It is important to recognize and monitor your habitual distractions. Likewise, it is also important to recognize and monitor your impulsive distractions, as well. For instance, say you get online to search for a specific topic or thing. You are almost done with your search and here comes a pop-up advertisement or an online notification. Pop-up advertisements and online notifications linked to email or social media accounts, are impulsive distractions. They are intended to grab your attention and derail you from your intended purpose.

Let's take another look at impulsive distractions. Compare these types of distractions to impulsive purchases when you go to the grocery store. When you go to the grocery store, you generally go with a purpose to buy specific food items, within a set budget and timeframe. You ever notice when you are ready to make a purchase and check out of the grocery store, you see more numerous small items for purchase at the checkout line. These items are generally the following: candy, lent rollers, gossip magazines and many other small items for sale. Similar to pop-up advertisements and online notifications, these small items for purchase at the checkout line are intended to derail you from your intended purpose. These small items are placed at the checkout line to distract you by enticing you to make additional, impulsive purchases. These impulsive purchases of small items can add up in costs, and time, thus slowing your productivity from your intended purpose.

Similar to you being derailed from your specific purpose at the grocery store, you can also be derailed from your specific purpose when you search online. Impulsive and habitual distractions can both be a bit tricky, if you do not recognize and monitor them. Overall, generally distractions can be complicated because they come in many forms, so take the time to recognize and monitor them. When you can recognize distractions, you have the power and choice to ignore distractions and focus on what is most meaningful. This allows you to fully focus on your intended purpose and substantive information.

Use

Similar to distractions, use of technology can be complicated, as well. Use of technology can be complicated depending on its application. When you use a computer or a smartphone, it provides you something in exchange, normally some sort of function. There is a level of dependency that it will perform based on your intended outcome from its use. However, some people become highly dependent and reliant on technology, such as smartphones and computers. Take the time to ask yourself if you are over-consuming technology? Let's look deeper into this.

We, as humans, have become fully computerized and digitalized. There is a great use of technology, but there is also great dependency on it, as well. Think of both the Internet and a television as windows in your home. You do not want to be left in the dark, so you open your blinds or windows from time to time to let light or fresh air in. But from time to time, especially while sleeping, you will close your blinds and windows. When you do open your blinds, sometimes there is an overload of things to view out of the windows all at one glance. When looking out of these windows, you can see what's going on, on the outside and you can view what others are doing. Furthermore, you can see what has changed or surfaced from the previous time you've looked out of the windows. You can see the flowers bloom and how the weather is. However, you can gain a deeper understanding and significance of all of this by actually going outside, living and experiencing it, as well. You can experience smelling and picking the flowers. You can enjoy and feel the temperature. You can engage in face-to-face conversations with others.

Similar to how we look out of windows, we also look at television and computer screens day by day to see what's currently going on. By turning off our television or closing our Internet browser from time to time, it gives us options in experiences and engaging in face-to-face conversations with others. When we look out of the window to judge the temperature, we perceive what it *appears* to look and feel like. When we would like to feel the temperature outside, but still remain inside the house by opening the window, we are still not getting the full experience. It is still hard to judge how the actual weather feels because our household temperature and window screen can alter the outside temperature and how much air is blowing inside. Thus, the only way to really feel the weather is to actually go outside and experience the temperature.

We can look out of the window and have our window open from time to time. Don't forget also to close the window and experience the outside, as well. Apply the same principle to browsing the Internet or watching television. We can look at the television and open the Internet browsers from time to time. However, do not forget to also turn off the television and close the Internet browsers from time to time to experience life, as well.

Sometimes we let technology and its tools dominate our thought process. We have become so dependent on our trusty smartphones to view and perceive everything that we turn to actual experience as a secondary choice. This dependency exists perhaps because of convenience, but it is not the same experience. In the context of computers and smartphones, it's really about developing a healthy balance of use and experience that prevents us from forming such a dependency on computers and smartphones.

Evaluate if you spend a lot of time trying to find that specific topic or something solely through technology on a daily basis. If this is the case, try to consider focusing on finding and creating your own moments of beauty through experience. Through experience, you can reach a higher level of clarity and understanding. In turn, this will allow you to deliberately tune into what is important and thus, allocate your time to what is most meaningful to you. When you allocate your time to focus on what is most meaningful to you and align it with your purpose, it can create an extraordinary impact on your life. When you develop the ability to *connect* your daily actions to what is most meaningful to you, to produce and deliver solutions, it will not only create an extraordinary impact on just your life, but others' lives, as well.

Part II: CONNECT

Connect One Idea to Another

Walls turned sideways are bridges.
- **Angela Davis**

What good is your ability to focus, if you cannot connect what you focus on to anything else? The core of Simplifyism encompasses the ability to connect what is meaningful to what is measurable. This means simply connecting one idea to another idea based off of information, patterns and experience. When you experience and recognize how information and ideas connect, then it becomes easier to create and consume information and ideas.

Whether it is complex information, ideas or occurrences, connection is the powerful bridge builder that links one's ability to focus on what is most meaningful to one's ability to process complex matter. Through connection, the walls of complexity can be turned sideways to create bridges to simplicity. Along these bridges to simplicity, one is able to recognize the common thread or consistent patterns to connect the dots. Having the ability to connect one idea or one piece of information to another is one level of understanding but one's ability to connect the dots in their life is a deeper level of clarity and simplicity.

Connecting the Dots

Steve Jobs, has a famous quote stating, "*You cannot connect the dots looking forward, you can only connect them looking backwards.*" Meaning, for what doesn't seem connected at the time in your life, try to take the time to look *back* and see how all of your successes and failures have helped shape and guide you to where you are today.

There is a story and meaning behind each circumstance or obstacle you face in your life. Throughout life, the experiences you have allow you to connect one circumstance to another. Each personal circumstance can be described as a *dot*. Each dot serves as a link that connects to another dot or circumstance. Within each of these dots, are clues and patterns that will enlarge your perspective and vision.

Steve Jobs' quote focuses on connecting the dots looking backwards. I agree with Jobs about the importance of connecting the dots in your life. I also agree that you can connect the dots looking backwards. However, I have to respectfully disagree with Steve Jobs on one part of that quote, and that is I *do* believe it is also possible to connect a few, not several, dots looking *forward*, as well. Now those dots looking forward may not be flawless or exact, however, you have some insight from looking backwards and drawing a connection to your current situation to establish a pathway forward to your next step or goal. By learning how to connect the dots looking backwards, you gain insight as to the common thread or consistent patterns throughout your life. This common thread or these consistent patterns are clues that have helped shape and guide you to where you are today. Connection is about finding the right patterns and combinations that speak to one another. Pattern recognition helps connect the dots by serving as a link that fills in the gaps and connects the disconnected. Identifying the common thread or consistent patterns throughout your life, helps you improve in making the connection to your next step or goal forward.

Recognizing the common thread or consistent patterns throughout your life, is important to connecting one circumstance or dot to another. This recognition includes an extensive thought process to determine how these dots connect and interact along the journey. So the big question is the following: *Are you at a point in your life, where you can recognize the common thread or consistent patterns to connect the dots?*

You will note that some of the dots are within your own control. Furthermore, those dots that are within your control can be studied to determine which dots are not essentially contributing to you making the connection to your next step or goal towards fulfilling your purpose. Try to take the time to examine if some of these dots can be possibly simplified.

Connecting the dots is critical to finding clarity to the complex problems you may face nowadays, from deciphering complex matter, to understanding the chaos in the world today. When you can connect one thing to another, you can see how things operate. This is a beautiful insight that can sharpen not only your intellect, but your instinct, as well. You can dot your i's and cross your t's, but what if they are still disconnected? It is about connecting *it* that truly matters. This is truly the key to understanding Simplifyism.

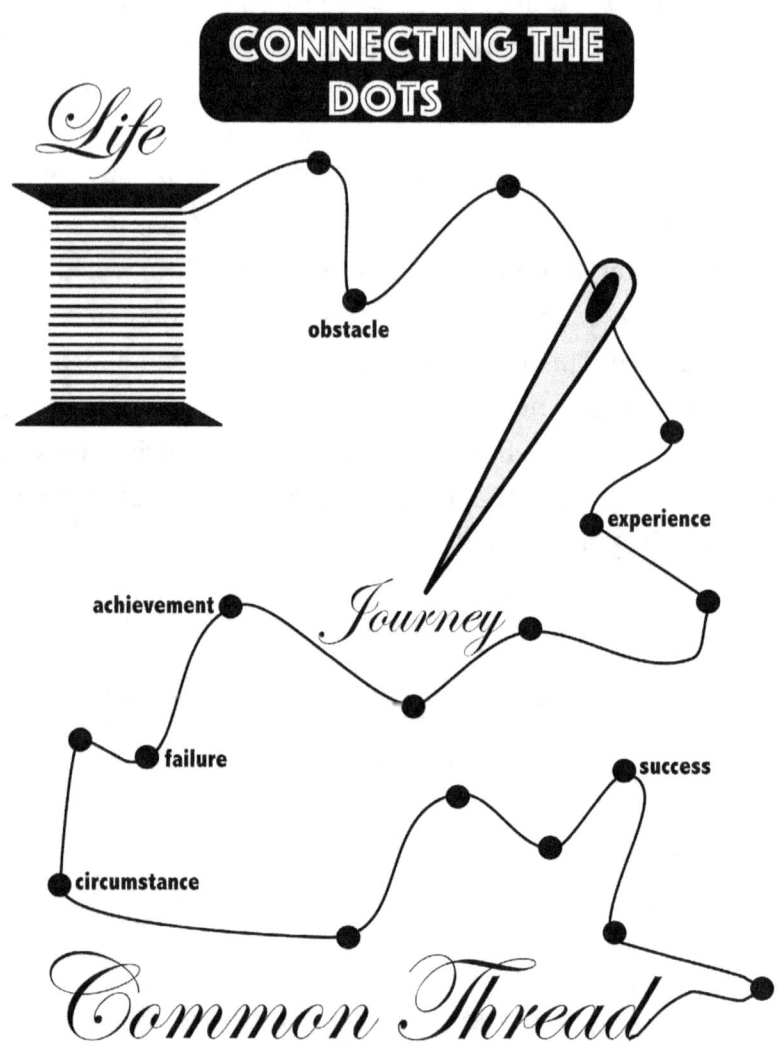

Power in the Small Things

Try to weave small actions into big patterns, in order to recognize these patterns and transform them into productivity.

One key element in connecting one idea to another is recognizing the power in the small things. There is power in the small things you do daily. Small actions performed daily are powerful catalysts for productivity, growth and change. Change starts in small increments and small prizes will be rewarded, that ultimately add up to grand prizes. However, it will take changing and adopting a new mindset and perspective, as well, to see how small actions have the ability to lead to a massive success. You have to consider a new mindset and change your perspective from focusing on the big and difficult to focusing on the small and attainable. This mindset coupled with small actions over a consistent period of time can produce positive, big results.

Try to weave your small actions into big patterns, in order to recognize these patterns and transform them into productivity. Focusing on the small goals along with the incremental details can make it easier to connect to the bigger goals at hand.

53

Today, we as humans scroll past and gloss over what we think are insignificant details in order to navigate through this chaotic world in which we live in. We are told to concentrate on the big and obvious things, and not to sweat the small stuff. However, it is the small things we do daily that makes a huge impact on not only our lives, but others' lives, as well. The key is to find the small but significant ways to achieve incremental improvements and apply them consistently over time.

Start by taking the time to reassess what you can possibly do different. Try to begin to look for tiny improvements you can make in your current situation or circumstances. Remember, Simplifyism is about focusing on what you already do have.

One powerful discipline you can practice is to spend a few minutes, at the end of each week, reviewing the things you did during the week that were successful and unsuccessful, or did not work. Then commit, each week, to make one concrete change to improve the things that did not work or were unsuccessful from the previous week. Develop this as a habit, and you will be amazed at its power and impact.

Making single small improvements each week builds momentum and over time has an extraordinary impact on your performance and results. These small habits are small actions that lay the foundation for success in your life. Examine the areas in your life that can be improved by making tiny adjustments or tweaks. Small tweaks can make big differences. Rather than immediately performing a complete 360 degrees turnaround or taking a big leap, look at taking tiny steps forward. Think of these tiny steps forward as small goals. Setting and achieving small goals can build your momentum and confidence.

Momentum is important because it will allow you to develop your own flow and rhythm. Over time, this momentum builds consistency and steadiness. The compound effect of performing an activity consistently, over time will help you make significant progress toward your goals. For instance, if you are a writer, write a page a day. If you are a basketball player, shoot ten free throws a day. If you are working, try to save $2.00 a day. No matter who you are, if you commit to the small goals over a consistent period of time, you will be amazed at how much you will accomplish.

In addition, as you establish your own groove and momentum, you will develop more confidence as you go along. There is power in celebrating small wins or successes because this gives you a sense of achievement and allows you to track closely your progress. The more small goals you accomplish, the more small wins you obtain under your belt. The more small wins you achieve, increases your belief in your ability to accomplish more. This confidence fuels your courage to move forward to attain your main, big goal. Each one of these small achievements can serve as a link to connect you to the next small goal. So, when you look back at these small goals, you will be able to see not only a chain of progression, but courage, as well. This courage will help you persevere in your pursuit of accomplishing your ultimate, main goal especially, when you encounter obstacles.

As stated before, there is power in doing the small things. However, there is more power in doing the *right* small things. When referring to the *right*, that means the best suited efficiently for the goal. Right is also about being selective in your choices.

How do you know what is right? Examine if what you are doing, is aligning with your purpose and contributing to you accomplishing your goal(s). Try to weave your small actions into big patterns, in order to recognize these patterns and transform them into productivity. This pattern recognition will allow you to connect to your main goal, dot by dot. When you are selective in your choices and work on the right, small things consistently, you will make significant progress toward your goals.

When you think of doing the right small things, keep in mind the act of setting the right goals for yourself. Try to set realistic and manageable goals for yourself. First, define the main goal. Then, break down the main goal into smaller, manageable goals. Smaller goals are easier to aim for, than bigger goals. Think of this process as how you would play a game of darts for the first time.

Playing darts is not easy. It requires practice, skill, technique and hand-eye coordination. There are plenty of areas to hit on the dartboard but you get the most points by hitting the dead center in a small circle, called the bull's eye. Think of your main, overarching goal as the bull's eye on the dartboard. When you aim your dart at the dartboard, always keep in mind hitting the main specific goal, the bull's eye. Similar to the game of darts, when you set and aim at the right, small goals, overtime with practice, your aims will keep getting closer and closer to hitting the main goal. Aiming at the right, small goals will help guide you to see how you are progressing and how you can improve to nail the bull's eye. Sharpen your skills and work through the small actions to attain the big goals.

Now, just think if you stood real close to the dartboard. Then you would probably instantly hit the bull's eye, because there is no challenge and it doesn't take much skill. However, that's a shortcut and cheating, if you stood close. By taking this shortcut, you will not develop the skills, techniques, or the coordination to attain your small goals and ultimately attain your main goal. You will not see the growth and the improvement, by taking shortcuts, but the further you step back from the dartboard, the harder it becomes. This is why the game of darts is played from a distance. The distance increases the challenge. It is through this challenge, you begin to diligently aim, develop and improve your skills.

Similar to the game of darts, in life, you should not take shortcuts to attain your goals. Instead, you should set and aim at the right, small goals and work at hitting those right, small goals first, before ultimately hitting the main goal. Remember though, if you aim for nothing, that is what you will hit, nothing.

When you do set the right goal, you want to envision this goal being achieved and firmly instill it in your subconscious. Take the time to write it down in a place where you can see it each day. Also, most importantly, write down how and when you are going to achieve it. This helps attract achievement of your goals into your life and what you need to make that vision a reality. It is one thing to set the right goals, but you also have to track your progress and create a measure of success. Reducing your goals to writing, and monitoring your progress is a powerful way to point yourself in the right direction and track your advancement.

When you do set and aim at your goals, it is normal to encounter obstacles along the way. Obstacles are hurdles that test your ability to continue to achieve your goals. Obstacles can slow down your progression and make it more complex than you anticipated. It is important to identify these complexities and their causation in order to continue making the connection to your goal(s) and working towards achieving success.

Goal Setting and Selectivity

Bull's Eye=Main Goal **Smaller Goal**

Goal Setting
DARTS

Complexity and Comprehension

Complexity is merely simplicity waiting to be connected.

We live in a world where everything is constantly changing and we have to quickly adjust and adapt to those changes. With change occurring at a rapid pace, information is constantly changing. In addition, how we deliver and explain this information is changing, as well. Despite, how much information is changing and becoming more complex, there is not much consideration given to the approaches on how to tackle the influx and complexity of constantly, changing information. Furthermore, there is not much consideration given to the approaches on how to *connect* constantly, changing information to others for comprehension.

Traditionally, people struggle with understanding information and ideas that are new or different. Most of us are great at starting new things, however it is a challenge for us to change our method of action. As humans, it is easy to be trapped in habitual and traditional approaches. Many times we do not even realize how habitual our approaches are to tackling complex problems and information. Most of the time, this is the major disconnect. When faced with complex information, most of us feel a bit overwhelmed and lose concentration quickly, which, by default, results in returning to traditional approaches and methods.

a. Complex Information and Data

Information and data are considered the golden keys these days, but without connection it falls flat for users and audiences. Today, the instantaneous lifestyle of social media creates impatient users and an audience who are accustomed to an immediate connection. However, trying to understand complex information and data and trying to connect complex information and data to others can be super challenging.

Information in itself can be pretty broad and diverse in subject matter. There are all types of information coming from multiple sources, which makes some content quite intimidating when looking at it on its surface.

With information being so broad and different, the concept of information becomes related to notions of communication, form, education, knowledge, meaning, understanding, pattern, perception and data. Multiple factors can influence the complexity of information. These factors may include the following: the content, language, purpose, structure, layout, interest, and level of familiarity or background knowledge. The same information can be complex in different ways, in different contexts, and of course, to different audiences. There is no one number or measure that can determine how difficult information is nor is there one solution to eliminating the complexity of information. As you can see the levels of complexity in information may vary and depends on the following factors: the subject matter, the individual's or audience's ability to comprehend, the circumstances, the accessibility to the information, how the information is written and how the information is communicated.

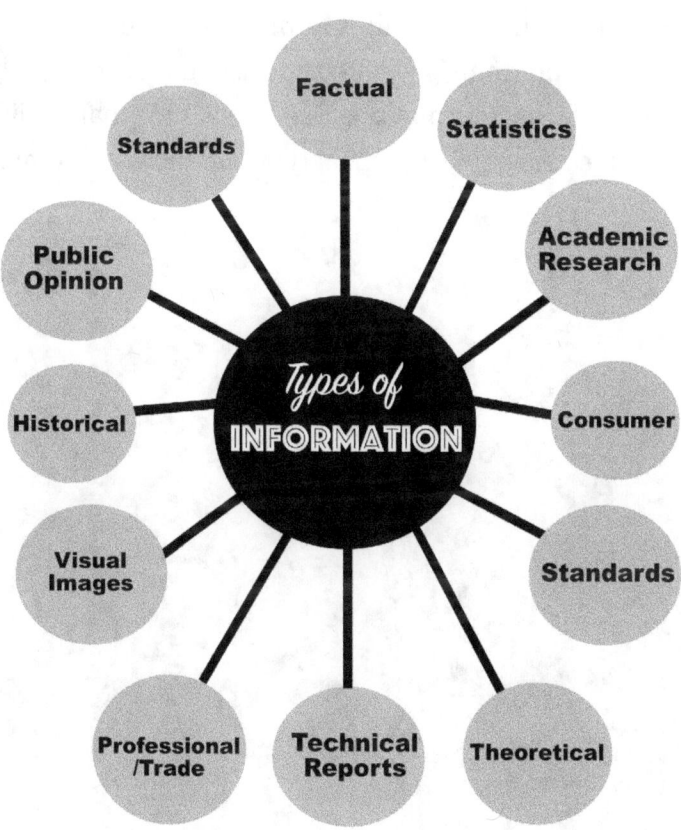

The types of information displayed above are not exhaustive.

Data are simply facts and figures, bits of information, but not information itself in its raw form. When data are processed, interpreted, organized, transformed, structured or presented so as to make them meaningful or useful, they are called information. Similar to information, there are all types of data coming from multiple sources. Also, data can be collected in many different formats. However, too many different formats can cause gaps in information and increase complexity.

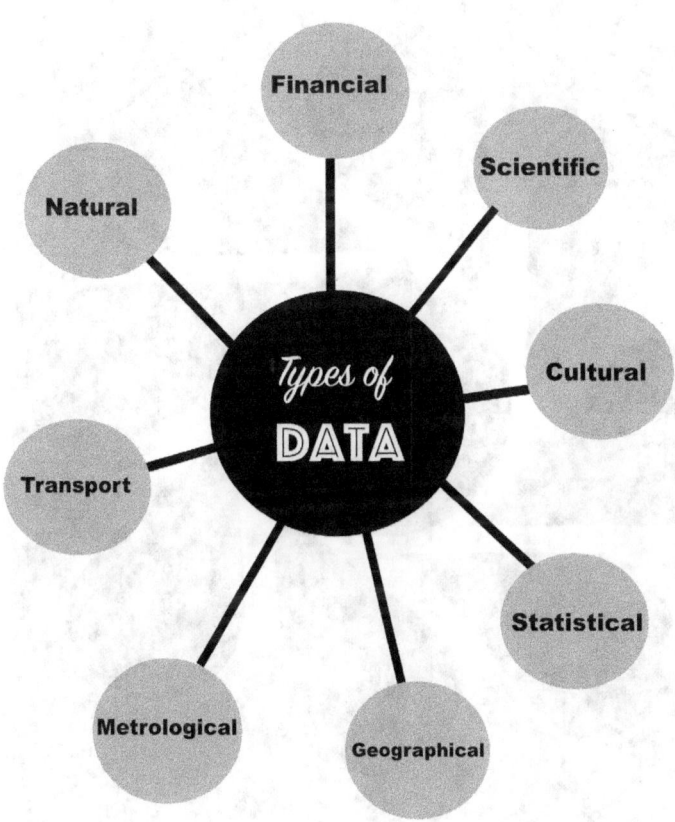

The types of Data displayed above are not exhaustive.

The sources of Big Data displayed above are not exhaustive.

On a daily basis, we are confronted with a lot of information. Trying to understand and connect this complex information can be challenging. Furthermore, trying to actually explain and deliver all of this complex information to someone else without completely confusing them can be even more of a challenge.

There is not one simple solution to prevent these complexities. However, simplicity is a key priority in tackling this vast amount of complex information from multiple sources. There is power in simplifying complex information to make it more comprehensible to others. Once one clearly frames simplicity as imperative and connect it to measurable goals, then one can begin combating complex information and seeing this information in a new light.

There are deeper and effective layers to combating and challenging the perception of complex information. Let's dive deeper into another, crucial layer of simplicity. Another important element of simplifying and connecting complex information is the act of breaking down information into its simplest form.

G. Eb Williams

b. Breaking Down Information Into Its Simplest Form

Considering the cognitive aspect the content of information demands, it is important to utilize an approach to simplify and connect such content. Breaking down information into its simplest form is just one of the many approaches to connecting information. When you break down complex information into its simplest form, it becomes easier to consume and digest.

Think of vegetable juicing or blending as an example. We all need our vegetables, however most of us do not like the taste of vegetables. Most of us know that vegetable consumption is essential to having a healthy lifestyle. But the taste and quantity of consumption is difficult for some. When we juice or blend vegetables, we break down its nutrients into liquid form to make it more digestible for easier consumption. Rather than eating each vegetable one at a time, which is time consuming and does not have the best taste, we have the option to juice or blend it. In order to reap the core benefits of vegetables, we can break down vegetables through the juicer or blender to simplify consumption and digestion of vegetables. Similar to the vegetable juicing or blending process, when we break down complex information into its simplest form it becomes easier to consume and digest. Thus, we are able to receive its core benefit, which is substantive information and sift out the useless, non-substantive information.

71

Complex Information

Juicer

Breaking Down Information Into Its
Simplest Form

Breaking down complex information into its simplest form consists of the following considerations:

1. Eliminate Distractions

Try to eliminate distractions and visual clutter, while trying to understand complex information. This allows you to focus and concentrate on just the information itself.

2. Consider the Purpose and the Message

Think about what the underlying theme, message or purpose is in such information. When reading, think about the message, the author is trying to convey to the audience. Once, you figure out the underlying purpose or message of such information, try to translate and explain that information into words that any person can understand.

3. Look at the Big Picture

When you begin to break down complex information, it is easy to get caught up in the minutiae. Take a moment to step back and look at it from a bird's view. The larger perspective or big picture may reveal that the complexities are actually simpler than you think.

4. *Break Down the Issue(s) or Topic(s) into Small Parts so that you can Look at Each Facet One at a Time*

Try to break down the issue(s) or topic(s) into bite-sized pieces to make it easier for the brain to digest new information. The reasoning behind this tactic is because the brain's working memory, which is where we manipulate information, holds a limited amount of information at one time.

5. *Tackle each Small Part of Complex Information into a Single Task*

Try to do one task at a time to prevent multitasking. Try not to perform multiple small tasks at the same time because it will defeat the purpose of breaking down the information or problem(s) into smaller parts. It may seem slow and nearly impossible at first. However, over time you will gain understanding and proficiency that will increase momentum.

6. Create a Visualization

Visuals can be very useful in problem solving and understanding complex information. A visualization serves as a pathway making it easier to move to the next task or issue, track progress and apply the necessary time allocation.

7. Jot Down and List the Parts or Issues that you do not Understand that may be Beyond your Direct Knowledge or Skillset

By identifying these issues upfront, you can resolve these issues before getting in waste deep.

8. Reword the Problem

Stating the problem differently often leads to different ideas. To reword the problem, look at the issue from different angles. Ask yourself the following questions: What is the roadblock here? Why is there a need to solve the problem? What will happen if the problem is not solved?

9. Seek Assistance from an Expert or a Professional

Ask for help from a professional who has more experience and knowledge with such information. Try to seek assistance from an expert regarding the problem, issue or information.

Even when you break down complex information into its simplest form, you still have to be able to connect such information to others. In order to connect information to others, it is imperative to display and communicate information in an easy, understandable way.

Take a look at both an hourglass and a digital watch. Both items have the same use and they both provide information. Both an hourglass and a digital watch, each contain over a hundred pieces, and perform the same function. With that being said, why create two products and methods that perform the same function? Well, the digital watch is more mobile and displays information in a digital format. The mobility and digitalization of the watch makes it more convenient and easier to read the time. On the other hand, if you look at an hourglass you see a way of breaking down time into its simplest form with the finest grain pieces of sand to display the time. A digital watch displays the time, as well. However, it displays the time in a simpler, calculated form by numbers and digits for easier comprehension.

This demonstrates that even if you break down information into its simplest form (piece by piece of sand per second), you still have to display and communicate information to others in an easy, understandable way. This helps others connect with such information. When you break down information into its simplest form, you have to consider how others or your audience will perceive and consume it. Those who have the ability to break down complex matter into its simplest form can make some complexities look simple. Furthermore, those who also have the ability to deliver and display complex matter into simple, yet understandable formats can transform some complexities into clarity.

c. Visual Communication Design

They say a picture is worth a thousand words. But when words are complex, pictures can be priceless.

One prominent way to communicate and display complex, textual information is through Visual Communication Design. Visual Communication Design (formerly graphic design) is a creative process that combines the visual arts and technology to communicate ideas and information. This particular area of design is about transforming ideas or messages into visualizations to inform, educate, or even entertain an audience. The idea behind visual design is not to invent a completely new story, but instead to tell the same story again in a new and interesting way. So when you combine and infuse visual communication with design it displays one level of familiarity and also displays another layer of unfamiliarity. This level of unfamiliarity makes it appear fresh, yet familiar and totally different at the same time.

Visual Communication Design illustrates new and fresh ways to display and communicate information, including data. Similarly, like the general idea behind Simplifyism, it is all about working with what you already do have. Visual Communication Design is about transforming, rearranging and connecting the information you already do have, but in a fresh, unique way.

As humans, we have to be creative in providing a mechanism to draw a connection to others or an audience. Each individual is different and unique in his or her own way. Thus, human connection mechanisms need to have more customization and a less rigid structure of traditional ways of thinking.

For instance, a custom visualization that conveys information is an important communication tool to map out a variety of systems of knowledge. We have to create powerful, visual illustrations to embody this human desire for meaning, order, balance, unity and symmetry. There is a shift in the way we try to conceive and consume human knowledge and information. We can see this shift in the way we try to understand the brain. Many think of the brain as a modular, centralized organ, where a given area is responsible for a set of actions and behaviors. However, when we look closer, we can see that the brain operates much like a symphony filled with hundreds of instruments, operating in one harmony to process various amounts of information.

65% of the world's population is made up of visual learners. Visualization is prevalent now due to the digitalization overflow on the brain, which demands a visual aspect to the information that is being consumed. In fact, visualization is unconscious. The eye is exquisitely sensitive to variations in color, shape and pattern. The language of the eye is through variations in color, shape and pattern. Now when you take the language of the eye and combine it with the language of the mind, which is about words, numbers, and concepts, you will begin to speak two languages simultaneously, both which enhance each other. The combination of both of these languages alters your perspective and changes your view of information.

Visualizing information transforms it into a landscape that you can explore in many different, new paths with your eyes. The ideas of grids, images, space alignment, colors, and typography are all captivating to the human eye, which speaks a language that is more comprehensible than most other languages. The challenge is that you have to navigate through dense information and if you are lucky, you may come across a clear path. This clear path, you may come across, is sometimes illustrated with beautiful graphic or data visualization, which is a relief.

Visualizing information helps clarify complex, textual information. Even when information is confusing, the visual depictions can likely bring clarity, which is beautiful. In addition, visualizing information is a form of knowledge compression. It is a way of squeezing and translating an enormous amount of complex information into an understandable format within a small space for better comprehension.

The Power of Visuals in Data

Today, we are facing complex and intricate challenges that cannot be understood by simply textual data, employing a diagram, chart, or a software program. When we look directly at raw data and numbers it appears to be just a lot of numbers and disconnected facts. When complex information and data are presented in raw form, they can be hard to explain and understand. However, when complex information and data are condensed and depicted visually, they become much easier to explain and understand.

Data, in particular, can be described as informative, interesting, yet broad and vague all at the same time. Data is scattered all around us and can be mined very easily. Data is the kind of resource that we can shape and design to provide new perspective and insights, which can lead to innovation and solutions. There is raw data and numbers being converted everyday by fancy software programs spitting it into fancy diagrams and charts. The question then becomes the following: How do we take this vast amount of scattered data and connect it to a human being?

Most humans learn through active participation. When a human being begins to work, play and experiment with data and information in a certain way, different patterns can be identified and revealed. It is still up to the human mind and eye to interpret patterns in fancy diagrams and charts. Seeing how data can be interpreted and transformed by humans into something beautiful can change a perspective.

Most people still try to explain and comprehend complex information and data through text form only. This has been the traditional default approach. When using solely this traditional approach, there is not as much consideration given to neither one's nor their audience's ability to focus, connect and process complex information, ideas and data. When communicating any form of information, the focus has to be on the audience's perception and their ability to understand such information. Your ideas are only as good as your audience's ability to understand them. *Good* ideas depend on originality, however, *Great* ideas depend on the ability of others to understand and connect with them. When you are explaining and delivering complex data, information or ideas, they need to resonate with the audience you are trying to serve. When creating visualizations, keep this in mind and you will see the benefits that Visual Communication Design can provide not only to you, but to others, as well.

The Benefits of Visual Communication Design

1. Visual Pattern Recognition

One benefit of Visual Communication Design is the ability to potentially recognize the less obvious and patterns that were otherwise scattered in only textual form. Connection is about finding the right patterns and combinations that speak to one another. Pattern recognition helps connect the dots by serving as a link that fills in the gaps and connects the disconnected. When we take the time to focus and visualize information, we begin to recognize patterns that are valuable.   When we start recognizing patterns in information, which would otherwise be scattered across other mediums, a new level of understanding surfaces. Once we recognize patterns within information, we can display these patterns by utilizing visual illustrations. Visual illustrations help simplify and effectively communicate pattern recognitions to an audience.

2. Saves Time in Explanation and Comprehension

Another benefit of Visual Communication Design is its unique ability to save time in the explanation and comprehension of information. Visual aids are more effective and more efficient than utilizing just solely textual formats. Instead of using several sentences of words to explain complex information, use a single picture to convey and illustrate a vast amount of information at one time. Through visual aids and images, the audience is likely to understand complex information quicker and far more clearly in a few glances, than when presented in just textual format.

People, particularly millennials, have short attention spans, which highlights the effects of an increasingly digitalized lifestyle on the brain. A 2015 study by Microsoft revealed that the average person's attention span in technology and social media is down to eight seconds, which is less than that of a goldfish. The average attention span for a goldfish is nine seconds. Thus, from research, a goldfish has a better attention span than humans. With that being said, the author or presenter has a tight window to quickly and clearly deliver their content to an audience, before the audience member's attention span drifts away. By utilizing visual aids, the author or presenter, can now get their point across quicker and more clearly without verbalizing text.

3. More Engagement and Retention

Visual Communication Design increases more engagement from an audience and increases more information retention from an audience, as well. These are extraordinary benefits of Visual Communication Design. Most people only tend to remember 10% of what they hear and 20% of what they read. However, people actually tend to remember 80% of what they see. Visuals deliver complex information more appealing than boring long sentences and paragraphs. By incorporating visuals into communication with an audience, there is a better chance the audience will be more engaged and the information will be retained more successfully, than through just text. Simply using our eyes more and visualizing information does wonders for the engagement and retention of information.

4. Flexible and Relatable

Visual Communication Design is more flexible and relatable than verbal communication, which is truly beneficial. In order to connect with an audience, it is important to create flexible, ingenious solutions that can relate to an audience. Visual aids have the ability to communicate ideas and information in multiple, dynamic and relatable ways. Most members of an audience come from diverse backgrounds. Within this diverse audience, there may be language and cultural barriers that are harder to overcome using solely verbal and textual communication. Unlike verbal and textual communication, visuals can communicate with an audience, despite cultural, geographical, ethnic or language differences among people.

5. Can Spark or Evoke an Emotional Response

Another benefit of Visual Communication Design is its ability to spark or evoke an emotional response in an audience. Visual Communication Design was created not only to answer questions, but to raise questions, as well. When you select or create visual images to illustrate an idea or information, you have to take human behavior into account. Consideration must be given to the emotional aspect of an audience.

As human beings, how we feel and how we react to what we see, is important because what we see resonates with us quicker than what we solely hear. When utilizing visual images, the presenter or author has the ability to evoke an emotional response on a tremendous level that mere words cannot. Visual Communication Design creates not only a visual impact on an audience, but an emotional impact, as well.

6. The Credibility of Information

Lastly, another benefit of Visual Communication Design is its ability to bring more credibility to information. There is a saying, *"Seeing is Believing."* What this means is that people place more belief in what they see. Whether it is information, data, a service, or a product, a visual image can reinforce the credibility of what you represent or what you present. When utilizing visuals, rather than just solely words, there is more consideration given to an audience's ability to consume and comprehend information.

How to Use Visual Communication Design

We have addressed both the importance and the benefits of Visual Communication Design. However, it is just as important to examine *how* to effectively use visuals and design to communicate complex information with an audience. Visual content is nothing without good design. No matter how great a message is, a poorly designed visual aid will not make much of an impact on an audience. In fact, a poorly designed visualization can deliver the wrong message, weaken content and confuse an audience. Many factors can contribute to a poorly designed visualization. For instance, some of these factors may consist of the following: cluttered layouts, confusing images, complicated texts, and illegible fonts. The best way to avoid a poorly designed visualization is to build a visual communication framework that follows the best design practices and methods.

One popular method of Visual Communication Design is creating an *infographic* (information graphic). An infographic is a graphic visual representation of information, data, or knowledge intended to present complex information clearly and quickly. Infographics can improve cognition by utilizing graphics to enhance the human visual system's ability to recognize patterns and trends. Moreover, this particular method can help simplify information and effectively communicate a complicated subject.

Example **Infographic** of Data Analytics

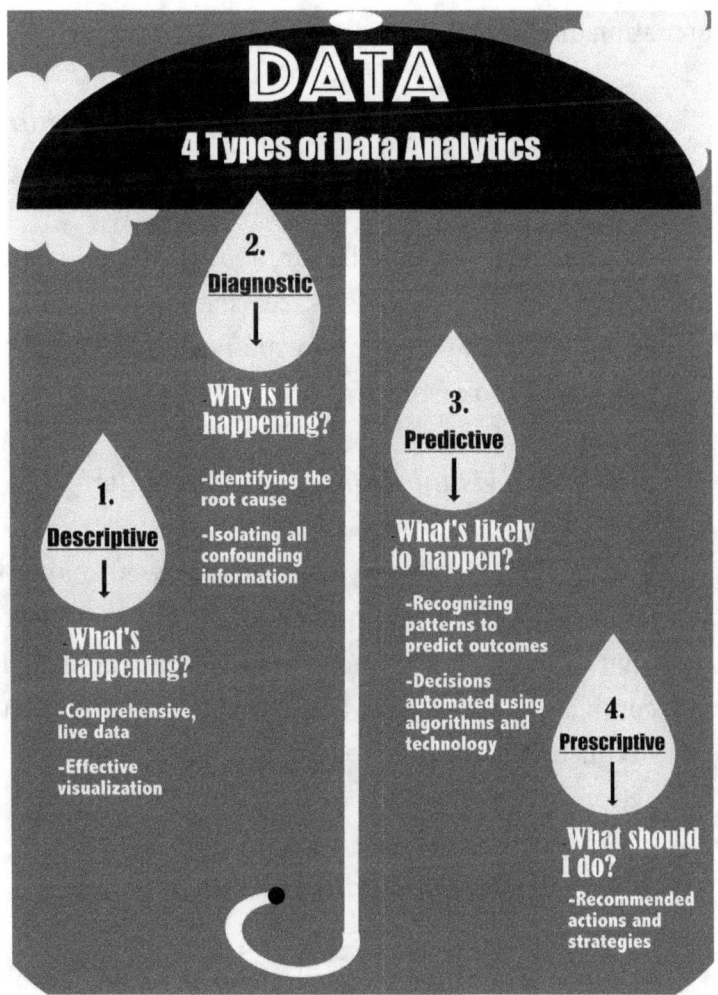

Here are some simple tools and tips on how to effectively create and utilize an infographic to explain complex information and data:

1. *Try to neatly arrange information into easy, digestible sections.*

All the sections can be unified with the same color scheme, which allows each section to stand alone successfully as its own informative guide, but yet create a cohesive look from afar.

2. *Create a visual pathway for the reader.*

Create a visual pathway by using arrowed shapes to lead the reader from an introduction of the subject to an invitation to learn more about the subject. This is compelling when you are dissecting complex subjects because it gives the reader a roadmap to your call of action.

3. *Use simple, but creative graphics.*

Make sure you use simple and creative graphics to create a strong and cohesive, design story.

4. Organize the information.

Organize and display the information in unique shapes to highlight and represent a topic.

5. Use interesting illustration, legible typography and different fonts.

Try to use interesting illustration, legible typography and different fonts to create an engaging infographic that draws the audience in and keeps their attention.

6. Use colors to break down an in-depth subject into easy, digestible parts.

Colors create a welcoming but authoritative vibe. Try to use the psychology of color to help you illustrate an idea or a key concept. According to the psychology of color, some colors have the ability to spark an emotion from an audience. For instance, try to use the following colors to create an emotion: Red=Passion, Blue=Trust, Yellow=Knowledge, and Green=Compassion. Use a white background or spaces, to counter balance the content and a lot of information. Also, try to create a pleasing contrast by using white text against a different bright or dark color background. The white text is crisp and attention grabbing in the most pleasing way.

These particular tips stated above are not exhaustive. However, these tips will provide you with some guidance in creating a correctly designed infographic. Furthermore, these tips will also help you in creating effective, visual content.

As previously stated, there is power in Visual Communication Design. Visual Communication Design combats the complacency of communicating and delivering complex information strictly in textual form only. When you convert complex, textual information into clear, understandable narrative by utilizing compelling visualizations, you can connect with an audience by giving them a fresh, creative perspective on the subject matter. Try to leverage an advantage over complex information by enhancing and simplifying the way you consume and communicate complex information. Try to utilize different visual options and approaches, so you will have more choices and possibly fewer limitations, which will allow you to create more while consuming less.

Creative Worthy

Creating more, while consuming less.

In this age of automation, half of the human workforce is expected to be replaced by robots and software in the next two decades. As machines take many of the jobs and perform them more efficiently, the only work left for humans is the kind of work that must be done creatively. However, creativity is not always encouraged inside or outside the workplace. Maybe this is because creativity requires a more in-depth analysis of looking at situations from different angles and perspectives. This means a possible change in traditional methods and approaches that have been used in the past. Creativity challenges these traditional methods by exploring new, innovative ideas and solutions to combat and conquer complexities.

Creativity is an important competency for seeking a pathway through complexity and connecting one idea to another. It is one thing to have an idea. However, it is another thing to translate this idea creatively, ultimately connecting it to the *right* audience, in the *right* way and at the *right* time. This is what you would call *creative translation*. In order to perform a creative translation, one must focus on connecting an idea or

95

information to an audience in not only a creative way, but also in an authentic way, as well. This is done by taking an honest and meaningful approach when translating an idea or information into a creative medium, such as a visualization. When one takes this approach, others are more receptive to the creative thought process involved in communicating and delivering the idea or information.

Creativity in itself seems to be complex until you take the time and realize it can be simplified, as well. When you think of creativity, you think of something new, yet original and unique. However, after the dissection of creativity, creativity is simply about making new connections to the unconnected. The connection can be taking something that already exists that is undervalued and connecting it by putting value into it. It can also be making a connection between two existing, yet different ideas or concepts. When you explore these types of new connections, your approach towards creativity is suddenly less intimidating and challenging. However, what is challenging is that you must discover your own creativity and innovation styles.

Creativity is about embracing our own authenticity, originality and individuality in a way that not only inspires others, but in a way that creates a meaningful impact, as well. We are all *creative worthy*, however, most of us ignore our creative instincts and abilities. Most of us fail to recognize when and how our creativity is stifled. Often times, we let fear, embarrassment and opinions prevent us from embracing and exploring our own creativity.

In order to explore this creativity and generate new ideas, we have to actively seek stimuli from unexpected places and then use these stimuli to build a connection. To seek stimuli from unexpected places, we have to use our imagination and envision possibilities in an elegant way that is results driven. When confronted with a creative roadblock, try to visually frame the problem and look at it from different angles. Recognize the leverage points and patterns to help connect to a solution. This is truly a creative way of connecting one dot to another.

G. Eb Williams

PART III: PROCESS

Process Complex Matter

It is a process to create more simplicity by consuming less complexity.

As human beings, our ability to creatively visualize problems and solutions can create quite an impact and a connection with others. It is how we *process* complexities internally that influences our instincts to fulfill our purpose and create a massive impact.

What exactly is a process? A process is a systematic series of actions or steps taken in order to produce something or to achieve a particular result. When we think about it, everything has a process. Whether it is getting ready for work or even simply making a cup of coffee. There is a process involved. It's not the sugar that makes the coffee sweet. It is the process.

When referring to a process in Simplifyism, it also encompasses a thought process. A thought process entails a sequence of decisions and exercising certain options. Pretty much given all the facts, what do you choose to selectively focus on, connect to and what is your thought process involved in this selectivity? Simplifyism is about unpacking a creative thought process in an honest and meaningful approach to empower people to expand and enhance how they process complexities.

As human beings, we are all wired differently in how we compartmentalize and filter ideas and information. We, as humans, process ideas and information different because we are all individually different, having our own unique capabilities and experiences. In addition, there are some factors that may influence how we approach and process ideas and information. These factors are the following: our background, age, gender, race, religion, sexuality, education and financial situation. Being realistic, some of us are denied a passage to privileges and are also denied access to opportunities. Some systems are designed to provide for and protect only some people but not all people. Some of us also do not have the privilege to let go of necessities. Furthermore, some of us lack the resources that are afforded to others. All of these factors can influence and contribute to how we process ideas and information as human beings.

Moreover, as humans, it is easy for us to be trapped in habitual processes. This can lead to problems and creating a default mindset of over processing and utilizing a quick solution first, before realizing the root of the problem. The root of the problem must be recognized and examined before trying to process the problem. There is also a tendency to try to process everything all at once. However, there is power behind processing one thing at a time instead of trying to process multiple things at a time.

Evaluating your processes, practices and approaches from time to time can help you gain a deeper understanding of how you process things. Taking the time to examine how you process things, such as complex information, can help you develop a calculated and systematic approach personally tailored to you to comprehend and conquer complexities. Furthermore, by evaluating how you process things, you can examine how you react to complex ideas and information.

Reactions

1. *Overreacting*

One of the most prevalent reactions when confronted with complexities is our ability to overreact. Overreacting is the most common default approach many of us take when we encounter complex situations and information. Overreacting is the act of interpreting a specific situation as being worse than it really is.

Many times when a problem occurs or when we think a problem has occurred, we have a tendency to look at all the possible negative or horrible things that *could* happen. Sometimes we have a tendency to magnify an issue or problem, when we do not take the time to think first before reacting to an issue or problem. For instance, I can remember a time in my life, where I myself overreacted.

One evening before heading to bed, I was flossing in between my teeth and I irritated my gums. My gums then began to bleed. I immediately washed my mouth out with mouthwash right after to try to eliminate the blood. At that time, I thought the mouthwash would indeed make my gums heal. I thought the problem was solved, so I went to sleep.

However, the next morning I woke up with a small amount of blood surrounding my tooth, which I had recently flossed the night before. I immediately ran into the bathroom and looked into the mirror. I quickly noticed that behind the crevices of that same tooth was what *appeared* to be a blood blister. I instantly went into panic mode. I then proceeded to research blood blisters online and its causes. This was mistake number one. I then took pictures of the "blood blister" and compared those pictures to the ones I found in my research online, which I strongly do not suggest nor encourage to anyone. This was mistake number two.

The next day, I went to work focusing on that same tooth, letting all the possibilities of this being a blood blister control my day. I was worried. I was looking at it every hour and treating it on my own, which again I strongly do not suggest. (*Do not treat any problem on your own. Instead, seek professional assistance from a qualified professional.*) I was terrified to go to the dentist because I was scared what they might find. I also didn't want to catch a hefty, expensive, dental bill. However, within the next two days, I eventually booked an appointment to the dentist.

The day of my dentist appointment, I was somewhat relieved knowing an answer was going to come about regarding this tooth. I spoke to the dentist and explained to her what happened. She then proceeded to take an x-ray, picture and examined the tooth. She pulled out her dental prong and picked at the tooth, only to find out my "blood blister" was actually a blueberry seed stuck behind my tooth. That's right a darn blueberry seed. It took her 2.7 seconds to remove the blueberry seed from the crevices of that tooth. I felt embarrassed and relieved all at the same time. That blueberry seed had me overreacting and worrying for hours, thinking it was a blood blister. I made a blood blister out of a blueberry seed. I realized thereafter I had lost a couple hours of sleep worrying about that tooth. I had invested several hours a day performing online searches, instead of just immediately booking a dentist appointment. In addition, I had spent money on home remedies and $369.00 at the dentist office over a blueberry seed and a small case of gingivitis. Talk about making a mountain out of a molehill.

My personal experience demonstrates how we first jump to the worst-case scenario or conclusion, when we encounter a problem or complex situation. Furthermore, I am also sharing my personal experience to show that I should have initially requested professional assistance from a qualified professional (dentist). Even when we don't have a problem, we can create a problem without even knowing it by overreacting or fearing the worst. Instead, we should ask a qualified professional to determine if there is a problem. If there is a problem, a qualified professional can possibly provide a solution.

Overreacting will not only waste your time, but will also waste your energy, as well. Try to be cautionary in how you expend your mental and physical energy because when you worry and get worked up over molehills (blueberry seeds), you will have less energy to tackle the more important matters in your life. It is not easy, but with practice and patience, you will develop more discipline in how you react to complex matter and difficult situations. One fundamental of building your mental strength and sharpening your thought process is adjusting your mindset to face any unprecedented event.

2. *The Over Traps*

When faced with unprecedented events and complex matter, we can sometimes create the hidden cause of complexities. Many times we are blind to our own reactions, which unnecessarily increase more complexity. Complexity inducing behaviors can be hard to identify and change, especially with an "Over" mindset.

An "Over" mindset is a mindset where you react or are stifled by *"Over Traps"* that prevent you from processing information and situations efficiently. These *"Over Traps"* are roadblocks that have the ability to steal your time, effort, and even the execution of your goals. These *"Over Traps"* all ironically overlap one another. We've already discussed one of the *"Over Traps,"* which is *Overreacting.* Now, let's examine some of the other *"Over Traps"* that can derail you from processing information and situations. Some of the other *"Over Traps"* includes the following:

1. ***Overconsumption***: Consuming something to an excessive level. An excessive level is the level beyond what is necessary.

2. *Overwhelmed*: A feeling or an emotion felt strongly in a great amount. It doesn't necessarily have to be positive or negative.

3. *Overvalue*: Placing too much importance and excessive value on something or someone.

4. *Overanalyze*: Analyzing something with too much detail and time.

5. *Overthink*: Thinking about something too much or for too long.

6. *Over process*: Processing something to a degree beyond its essential purpose.

7. *Overlook*: Failing to notice something.

8. *Over promise*: To promise more than can be delivered.

9. *Over share*: To disclose too much or too many details about something or someone.

10. *Overcompensate*: Taking excessive measures in attempting to correct or make amends for an error, weakness or a problem.

11. *Overestimate*: Estimating something to be better, larger or more important than it really is.

12. *Overload*: To load to an excessive amount.

13. *Overboard*: Going to the extremes, especially in regard to the approval or disapproval of a person or a thing.

There are many more "Over Traps;" however, this is just some of the most common "Over Traps" that can derail you from processing information and situations. When you overvalue the "Over Traps," you then undervalue how you process complex matter and situations. Try to take some time to recognize and really understand the "Over Traps." By recognizing and understanding how the "Over Traps" impact your reactions to complex matter, you can adjust your mindset. When you feel overwhelmed with complex information or matter, try to lose the "Over" mindset and simply start over. Remember the only "Over" that is undervalued and underrated is starting over.

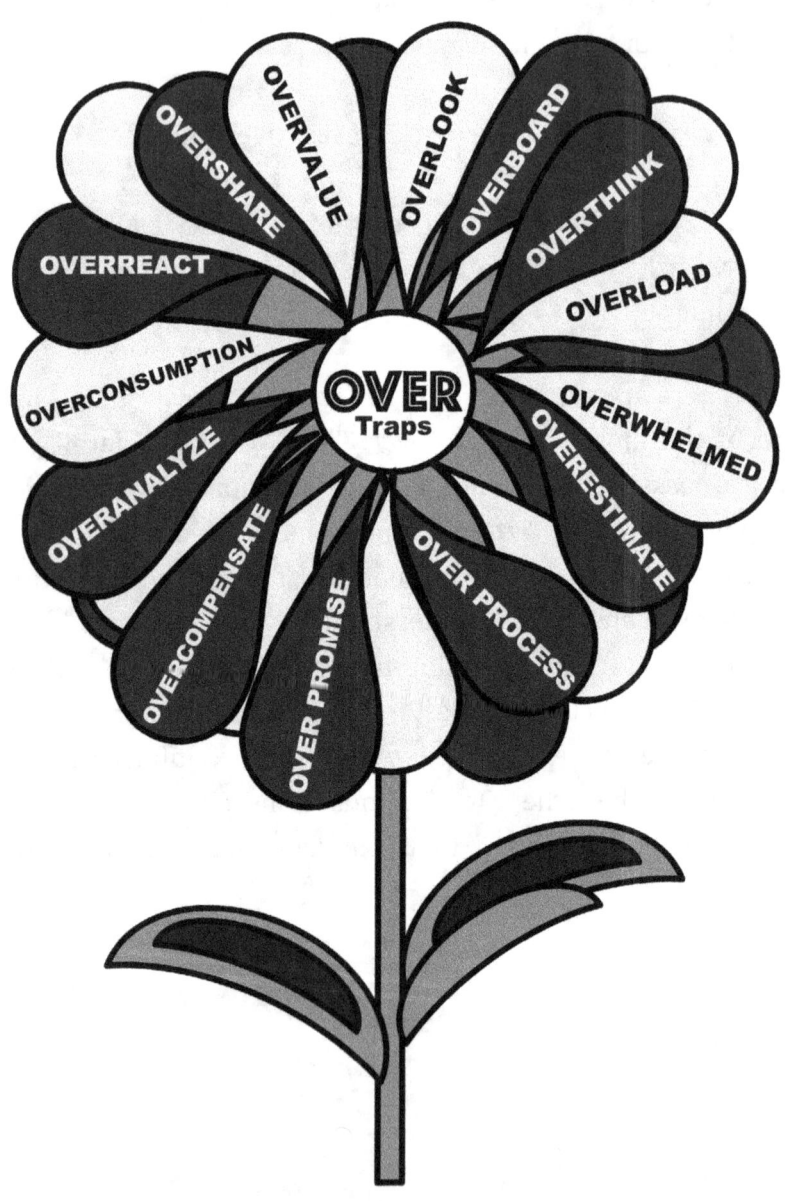

Failure is Part of the Process

Today, failure is a common occurrence in our unpredictable and uncertain world. It is a natural part of human existence. Failure can be defined as the lack of success in doing or achieving something. However, failure is not always bad.

In fact, there is authentic and memorable wisdom that is derived from failure. Each failure you experience provides you with valuable information and knowledge. You see failure can even change your perspective on success. Just think if you have failed at something in your life that means you have at least tried or performed something. Finding success through experiencing failure is success in its own being because at least you tried and took action. When you do experience failure, ask yourself the following question: Would I rather have an "oh well" or a "what if?" With an "oh well," you may have failed but you do have an answer. You know if you would like to try it again, or what you could've done different so on your next try, you can correct it. However, with a "what if" you are still in the dark because you do not know what the outcome is or what it could have been.

There is a saying, *"sometimes you have to lose, to win again."* This means failure is a necessary by-product of success. So why is failure always shortchanged? Maybe because if we dive deeper into failure it is emotionally unpleasant and toys with our self-esteem. Sometimes we also do not want to think about failure because it only makes us replay why and how we went wrong. Perhaps we all prefer our existing beliefs to be favored rather than alternative explanations. We also tend to downplay our responsibility and do not want to take ownership of what went wrong. It is interesting how people who experience failure, sometimes blame the reasons for failing on external or situational factors, only to do the reverse when assessing the failures of others.

There are an infinite number of reasons for why we fail. Some reasons for failures arc the following: lack of preparation, inattention, process inadequacy and complexity, lack of training or ability and uncertainty. Examining and analyzing our failures requires, patience and being honest with ourselves. Furthermore, it requires an in-depth reflection to learn from failures in order to improve for future performance. To learn from failures, it takes time to process and understand it. When we take the time to process and understand failures, it can be our greatest teacher and strength because every failure conveys valuable information. However, the real challenge lies in our ability to recognize this valuable information and make the necessary corrections or adjustments to overcome failures.

Failure is about deconstructing mistakes, and learning from these mistakes to see what works well and what does not work. To learn from each failure, you have to examine what went wrong and systematically analyze it until you understand how it went wrong.

It is also important to simplify each one of your failures you've experienced in life. One way to help in simplifying your failures for improvement is by categorizing each failure. By categorizing each failure you've experienced, you will notice that some failures are easier to grasp and recover from than others. In addition, you can then make the necessary corrections and adjustments to overcome such failures. For the purposes of learning and improvement, categorize each one of your failures by looking at all of your failures you've experienced in life and separate the "Snapback" failures from the "Long Shot" failures.

"Snapback" failures are the types of failures that come close to success. Pretty much you were on the right track and came close to success, but you came up a little short. With these types of failures, you can snapback or rebound with some minor tweaks within a comfortable period of time to achieve success.

On the other hand, "Long Shot" failures are the types of failures that do not come close to success. You've missed success by a long shot. These failures take a deeper analysis as to what went wrong. These types of failures require more time to examine and also require much more than just a tweak to achieve success.

Now sometimes you may have experienced a failure that is in between a "Snapback" failure and a "Long Shot" failure. You didn't miss success by a long shot but you also didn't come close to success. These types of failures are called, "Brick" failures. Sometimes, it is good when you experience these types of failures because you can really examine where you went wrong from the beginning to the end, yet you have some level of confidence from not completely missing success from a long shot.

There is a quote by Rick Barry that says, *"You will miss 100% of the shots you don't take."* What this means is success is achievable only to those who actually take action. Now lets use the game of basketball as an analogy and as an example to look further at the different types of failures.

When it comes to failures consider "Long Shot" failures as "Air Balls" in the game of basketball context. These are the types of shots that miss the rim and backboard completely because one either undershoots or overshoots the basketball. "Air Balls" are harder to rebound from because they do not hit anything. Now lets take a look at the "Snapback" failures.

These types of failures can be compared to the types of shots that can be easily tipped back into the hoop, like "Tip-ins" in the game of basketball context. These are the types of shots where the ball bounces in and out of the hoop, or bounces off of the rim. Lastly, there are "Brick" failures. These types of failures can be compared to "Brick Shots" in the game of basketball context. These are the types of shots where one either misses the rim but hits the backboard or hits the rim in a very ugly way. All in all, with all of these different types of basketball shots just described, the basketball does not go into the hoop on the initial attempt.

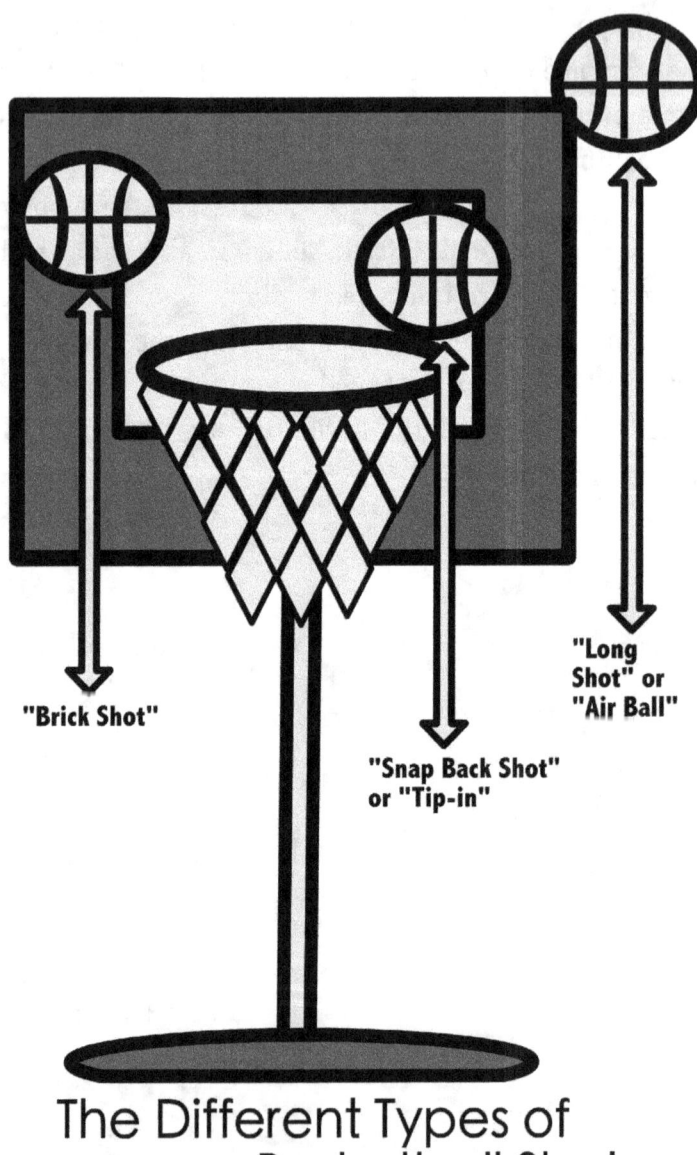

"Brick Shot"

"Snap Back Shot"
or "Tip-in"

"Long
Shot" or
"Air Ball"

The Different Types of
Missed Basketball Shots

As you see, all these types of missed basketball shots are not the same. Similarly, all failures are not the same, as well. Some failures are easier to grasp and recover from than others. So why should you examine, analyze and categorize your failures you've experienced in life? Because it is just as important to examine, analyze and categorize our failures (failure dots) as much as we do our successes (successful dots) that we've experienced in life.

Failures and successes work hand in hand. Both are a part of the process and the journey in life. All in all, instead of worrying about failure, replace that worry with a new paradigm by recognizing the inevitability of failure in today's complex world. The key to this paradigm is that you have to reframe how you define and treat failure. Try to learn from each failure and try again. The sooner you look back and reflect at your failures, the more time you will have to correct and improve where you went wrong. It may be challenging to recover after failure, however it can be rewarding, as well. It takes time to recover after failure. Nonetheless, it takes courage to overcome failure and ultimately achieve success.

G. Eb Williams

Simply Courage

Courage is the most important of all the virtues, because without courage you can't practice any other virtue consistently.
- Maya Angelou

Courage is a unique quality that enables one to face and confront fear, uncertainty, and difficulty. Courage comes from the heart, mind, and spirit. Courage is neither an intellectual quality, nor can it be taught in the classroom. Instead, courage is generally gained through multiple experiences involving risk-taking, criticism and hardships. Hence, developing and exercising one's courage is a powerful process in itself.

It takes courage to achieve success. You see courage and success go hand in hand. Success can be defined in many different ways or perspectives. However, one common quality that is needed to achieve success is courage. It takes courage to make bold moves and go against the grain of what others are doing. It is your courage that strengthens your tolerance for the discomfort you face in life, whether this discomfort stems from a failure or just plainly stepping outside of your comfort zone.

119

The courage to confront your own failures and imperfections is crucial in how you process things. *"Trust the process,"* is a phrase used when one faces circumstances that are sometimes uncontrollable and beyond his or her reach. Courage is actually what gets you to trust the process and enjoy the journey. When you learn to trust the process through exercising your own courage, then you can push yourself beyond what you thought were your limitations. Many of us doubt ourselves everyday because we doubt our own courage, knowledge, and potential. Do not doubt what you already do know, instead embrace and simplify what you do know through your own courage. Try to find your own courage from within and utilize it to capitalize on fears and uncertainties as doorways of opportunity. It is not easy. In fact, it takes time to develop courage and it is a powerful process in itself. However, once you develop and exercise your own courage it then becomes easier to process complexities and maximize your potential. Furthermore, you are able to redirect your valuable attention towards what is most meaningful, which in turn enables you to achieve more by doing less.

Conclusion

The most common way people give up their power is by thinking they don't have any.
-Alice Walker

From time to time, you have to ask yourself if you are sacrificing your power, in exchange for your reactions to complexities? There will always be some challenges you will face in life. The key to whether you succeed and overcome these challenges is in how you *choose* to rise above them. Some complexities you may encounter in life are uncontrollable, however, how you choose to react and process some of these complexities can be controllable. There are some valuable approaches and options available in tackling some complexities. You just have to try to process these complexities, dot by dot, into its simplest form.

There is no one solution to simplicity. However, just knowing you have a choice to control your reactions is power in itself to improving simplicity. This power can help you elevate your potential by simplifying complexities with purposeful actions and eliminating distractions. Utilize your power to take control over your actions and reactions when you are confronted with complex matter.

121

Try to connect on your existing strengths, skills, and talents to create and define your own path to success. Take the time to systematically focus, connect and process the dots along your own path to success. You will be surprised of the potential opportunities you can creatively explore based off of what you already do know, have, and are capable of. That is Simplifyism at its best.

About the Author

G. Eb Williams,
Human, Believer, Illustrator, Photographer, Writer, Attorney

G. Eb Williams writes, speaks and teaches on the importance of simplicity and time-management. She has extensive knowledge in simplifying complex matter through digestible, visual graphic illustrations and presentations. She understands the balance of creating and illustrating a visualization of complex matter, while meeting today's increasingly, demanding challenges.

www.simplifyism.com
www.gebwilliams.com

Acknowledgements

First and foremost, thank you God for planting these seeds within me to grow, to flourish and to share with others.

There are no words to describe my enormous gratitude to my Mother. She is the most courageous person I know and my role model. I thank her for her patience, support and motivation throughout the writing and revision processes.

Thank you Yonie for believing in me. I am forever grateful for your encouragement and support.

Thank you to the reader. I wrote this book to simply try to expand what is possible in an individual's potential. I have always had a fascination with simplicity, design and human connection. There is an impact in creating connection through simplicity and design, and the unique impression it leaves on people.

I personally love to transform complex matter, such as information and data, into beautiful, simple visualizations that reveal hidden patterns and unexpected connections. I enjoy finding hidden patterns to improve productivity and time-management. I try to use simple, elegant ways to view and understand complex matter, including information. One way to navigate through this information overload, and highlight the hidden patterns is through Visual Communication Design. By writing this book, I hope to inspire others by revealing unexpected insight on how we process complex information, ideas, and even certain occurrences. Ultimately, it may just change the way we see the world.

I thank you for reading and investing your time and energy.

One love,

G. Eb Williams